Emersyn's Story:
A Book About Juvenile Arthritis

Written by: Laurie Vineberg Buch

Illustrated by: Alanna Walsh

Just For You

Emersyn's Story: A Book About Juvenile Arthritis

Copyright © 2019 by Laurie Vineberg Buch. All rights reserved.

No rights claimed for public domain material, all rights reserved. No parts of this publication may be reproduced, stored in any retrieval system, or transmitted in any form or by any means, electronic, mechanical, recording, or otherwise, without the prior written permission of the author. Violations may be subject to civil or criminal penalties.

ISBN:
978-1-63308-476-6 (paperback)
978-1-63308-477-3 (ebook)

Interior Design by *R'tor John D. Maghuyop*
Illustrated by *Alanna Walsh*

CHALFANT ECKERT
PUBLISHING

1028 S Bishop Avenue, Dept. 178
Rolla, MO 65401

Printed in United States of America

Emersyn's Story:
A Book About Juvenile Arthritis

Written by: Laurie Vineberg Buch
Illustrated by: Alanna Walsh

Thank you…

I would like to offer a heartfelt thank you to everyone involved in Emersyn's journey thus far. The amazing staff in the Rheumatology department of the MUHC in Montreal. In particular, Dr. Rosie Scuccimarri, who is one the most compassionate doctors we've had the pleasure of being treated by, along with her nurses Nadia Narducci and Charlene Hopper.

I'd also like to thank my friends and family, especially my husband Shannon for supporting my decision to persist to find a diagnosis for all those months, and my other children Averie and Austin for being such amazing siblings to Emersyn and so understanding to all the time it has taken to get her well again.

Lastly I would like to thank Emersyn for being the brave, strong, beautiful princess warrior that she is! You make it so easy to be your mom and I couldn't be prouder to be on this journey with you. I love you.

Xox
Natalie (Emersyn's mommy)

Dear Emersyn,

This book was made for you to know about something you have had since you were 4 years old. It is called systemic juvenile arthritis and people all over the world have it.

Lots of kids need to take medicine and see doctors. When they are old enough, they learn why. You have shown us that you are an amazing girl and we feel you are ready to learn about your arthritis.

This book will talk about juvenile arthritis but also it talks about how we are so proud of you and all your bravery beads. We hope this book will help answer your questions, always know Mommy and Daddy are here for you and you can always come to us to ask questions or talk about your arthritis.

Arthritis is something that people of all ages have. Older people have it and some kids do, too. Arthritis means your bones or joints hurt. You have bones and joints in your hands, arms, legs and feet. When your joints hurt and you have trouble coloring, running or going up the stairs, it can be because of your arthritis.

If you feel your fingers, toes, wrists, knees or ankles hurting a lot, a good thing is to tell Mommy or Daddy. You might need special medicine. Arthritis is something people have and it is only a small part of who they are. With medicine, a lot of people don't feel any of the pain and can do everything they want to do.

Medicine comes in different ways, you are sooo cool because you swallow pills. I don't think any of your friends can do that. It's a special skill! Swallowing pills is one way to take medicine. Another way is needles, like our special Saturday injections that we do at home. You help me take my medicine and it shows what an amazing and kind daughter you are. You are only 5 years old but you already know how to take medicine like teenagers and adults…so cool!

Here are just a few people you know that also take medicine, for many different reasons.

Daddy, Bubby, Grandpa and Austin- they all take pills to help them just like you!!!

Averie and Austin are so proud to have a sister like you. They love laughing with you and playing family. You make us all smile with your cuddles and jokes. Daddy loves playing games and reading with you and Mommy loves eating new foods and shopping with you. We are all so so so so lucky to have each other!

Sometimes we need to go to the hospital for check ups or tests. We go for blood tests or pokes once a month. This is to check if the medicine is working well. Believe it or not, the doctors get a lot of information from the blood test. It's like getting a book on what is happening inside your body, pretty amazing. The poke isn't fun, but we've learned the way you feel most comfortable. We always remember you don't need a band aid. The poke or blood test doesn't take long, and the best part is you get another bravery bead. You deserve it! *

* Bravery Beads are an extra long necklace that we add a bead to every time you do anything at the doctor. From an appointment to a blood test, anytime you show bravery you get to add a bead. Bravery beads are given for needles, taking pills, x-rays, occupational therapy, physical therapy, and special events.

You see a few different doctors. Some doctors are regular doctors, ones that Leni, Hadley, Eva and Mayan go to. They go for check ups and see them when they have coughs or colds.

You have Dr. Rosie. She is the rheumatologist, that means she is an expert in arthritis. She is the one making sure the medicine is doing a good job!

Sylvie, our Occupational Therapist or OT, is someone that helps make sure your muscles are strong. You also get to visit the eye doctor, he checks your eyes- just like all the other kids.

They all care so much about YOU! How lucky are we to have so many people that care about you?? But really who wouldn't, you are one awesome kid!!!

In our family there are so many people that love you, not only because you love to swim, dance and do sticker puzzles, but also because you are a kind and caring person. Anyone would be lucky to be close to you. Bubby, Zaidie, Grandma and Grandpa love watching you grow up. Grandma, Zadie and Bubby also visited the hospital a lot in the last little while, so they know what it's like. ☺

We hope this book has helped answer some questions you have. You can always look at it when you need, it is always here for you. Juvenile arthritis is just a SMALL part of you. Emersyn, you are a wonderful kid and yes you have arthritis but what we have learned is that you are strong and brave. You have a wonderful smile and laugh and it makes everyone happy, even Patches. We love you to the moon and back!

So remember these important things:
1. You have juvenile arthritis which means you can get pain in your toes, fingers, wrists, ankles and knees.
2. If you feel very tired, or have trouble coloring or walking, just let an adult know.
3. You take medicine for your arthritis, but many people all over the world take medicine for different reasons.
4. You have a big family that loves you and friends that are lucky to have you. We are all in this together!
5. You are kind ,caring, funny and the best cuddler!!!!

WE LOVE YOU!!!
Love Mommy, Daddy, Averie, Austin and Patches

Proceeds raised from this book will go to the following organizations:

Montreal Children's Hospital Rheumatology Department
www.thechildren.com

Montreal Children's Hospital Neurology Department
www.thechildren.com

Books That Heal
www.booksthatheal.org

www.ingramcontent.com/pod-product-compliance
Lightning Source LLC
Chambersburg PA
CBHW042027150426
43198CB00002B/94